SOME MAJOR EVENTS IN WORLD WAR II

THE EUROPEAN THEATER

1939 SEPTEMBER—Germany invades Poland; Great Britain, France, Australia, & New Zealand declare war on Germany; Battle of the Atlantic begins. NOVEMBER—Russia invades Finland.

1940 APRIL—Germany invades Denmark & Norway. MAY—Germany invades Belgium, Luxembourg, & The Netherlands; British forces retreat to Dunkirk and escape to England. JUNE—Italy declares war on Britain & France; France surrenders to Germany. JULY—Battle of Britain begins. SEPTEMBER—Italy invades Egypt; Germany, Italy, & Japan form the Axis countries. OCTOBER—Italy invades Greece. NOVEMBER—Battle of Britain over. DECEMBER—Britain attacks Italy in North Africa.

1941 JANUARY—Allies take Tobruk. FEBRUARY—Rommel arrives at Tripoli. APRIL—Germany invades Greece & Yugoslavia. JUNE—Allies are in Syria; Germany invades Russia. JULY—Russia joins Allies. AUGUST—Germans capture Kiev. OCTOBER—Germany reaches Moscow. DECEMBER—Germans retreat from Moscow; Japan attacks Pearl Harbor; United States enters war against Axis nations.

1942 MAY—first British bomber attack on Cologne. JUNE—Germans take Tobruk. SEPTEMBER—Battle of Stalingrad begins. OCTOBER—Battle of El Alamein begins. NOVEMBER—Allies recapture Tobruk; Russians counterattack at Stalingrad.

1943 JANUARY—Allies take Tripoli. FEBRUARY—German troops at Stalingrad surrender. APRIL—revolt of Warsaw Ghetto Jews begins. MAY—German and Italian resistance in North Africa is over; their troops surrender in Tunisia; Warsaw Ghetto revolt is put down by Germany. JULY—allies invade Sicily; Mussolini put in prison. SEPTEMBER—Allies land in Italy; Italians surrender; Germans occupy Rome; Mussolini rescued by Germany. OCTOBER—Allies capture Naples; Italy declares war on Germany. NOVEMBER—Russians recapture Kiev.

1944 JANUARY—Allies land at Anzio. JUNE—Rome falls to Allies; Allies land in Normandy (D-Day). JULY—assassination attempt on Hitler fails. AUGUST—Allies land in southern France. SEPTEMBER—Brussels freed. OCTOBER—Athens liberated. DECEMBER—Battle of the Bulge.

1945 JANUARY—Russians free Warsaw. FEBRUARY—Dresden bombed. APRIL—Americans take Belsen and Buchenwald concentration camps; Russians free Vienna; Russians take over Berlin; Mussolini killed; Hitler commits suicide. MAY—Germany surrenders; Goering captured.

THE PACIFIC THEATER

1940 SEPTEMBER—Japan joins Axis nations Germany & Italy.

1941 APRIL—Russia & Japan sign neutrality pact. DECEMBER—Japanese launch attacks against Pearl Harbor, Hong Kong, the Philippines, & Malaya; United States and Allied nations declare war on Japan; China declares war on Japan, Germany, & Italy; Japan takes over Guam, Wake Island, & Hong Kong; Japan attacks Burma.

1942 JANUARY—Japan takes over Manila; Japan invades Dutch East Indies. FEBRUARY—Japan takes over Singapore; Battle of the Java Sea. APRIL—Japanese overrun Bataan. MAY—Japan takes Mandalay; Allied forces in Philippines surrender to Japan; Japan takes Corregidor; Battle of the Coral Sea. JUNE—Battle of Midway; Japan occupies Aleutian Islands. AUGUST—United States invades Guadalcanal in the Solomon Islands.

1943 FEBRUARY—Guadalcanal taken by U.S. Marines. MARCH—Japanese begin to retreat in China. APRIL—Yamamoto shot down by U.S. Air Force. MAY—U.S. troops take Aleutian Islands back from Japan. JUNE—Allied troops land in New Guinea. NOVEMBER—U.S. Marines invade Bougainville & Tarawa.

1944 FEBRUARY—Truk liberated. JUNE—Saipan attacked by United States. JULY—battle for Guam begins. OCTOBER—U.S. troops invade Philippines; Battle of Leyte Gulf won by Allies.

1945 JANUARY—Luzon taken; Burma Road won back. MARCH—Iwo Jima freed. APRIL—Okinawa attacked by U.S. troops; President Franklin Roosevelt dies; Harry S. Truman becomes president. JUNE—United States takes Okinawa. AUGUST—atomic bomb dropped on Hiroshima; Russia declares war on Japan; atomic bomb dropped on Nagasaki. SEPTEMBER—Japan surrenders.

WORLD AT WAR

Invasion of Poland

WORLD AT WAR

Invasion of Poland

By G. C. Skipper

Consultant:
Professor Robert L. Messer, Ph.D.
Department of History
University of Illinois at Chicago

 CHILDRENS PRESS, CHICAGO

Signing of the Versailles Treaty

28834

FRONTISPIECE: A photo of Adolf
Hitler from Eva Braun's collection.

Library of Congress Cataloging in Publication Data

Skipper, G. C.
  Invasion of Poland.

  (World at war)
  Includes index.
  Summary: Describes the events leading up to the
German invasion of Poland in September 1939.
  1. World War, 1939–1945—Campaigns—Poland—
Juvenile literature. 2. World War, 1939–1945—
Poland—Juvenile literature. 3. Poland—History
—Occupation, 1939–1945—Juvenile literature.
[1. World War, 1939–1945—Campaigns—Poland.
2. Poland—History—Occupation, 1939–1945]
I. Title. II. Series.

D765.S555 1983   940.54'21   83-7634
ISBN 0-516-04775-2

PICTURE CREDITS:
U.S. ARMY PHOTOGRAPH: Cover, pages
4, 20 (top), 37, 45
HISTORICAL PICTURES SERVICE, INC.:
Pages 6, 9, 17, 28
UPI: Pages 8, 10, 11, 12, 13, 15, 16, 18,
19, 20 (bottom), 21, 22, 23, 24, 25, 27,
30, 31, 33, 34, 37, 38, 39, 40, 42, 43, 44,
46
LEN MEENTS (Maps): Pages 9, 17, 28

COVER PHOTO: German soldiers
parade through the streets of Warsaw.

PROJECT EDITOR
Joan Downing

CREATIVE DIRECTOR
Margrit Fiddle

In 1919, after the end of World War I, a peace treaty was signed at Versailles, near Paris. The winning nations—mainly Great Britain, France, Italy, and the United States of America—severely punished a defeated Germany.

The Treaty of Versailles declared that Germany had been solely to blame for starting the war. It redrew the map of Germany, giving away or splitting up much of her territory. Alsace-Lorraine, for instance, became part of France. The Malmédy area became part of Belgium. The Rhineland was occupied by troops from the winning nations.

The Prussian port city of Danzig (above) was taken from Germany after World War I.

Much of the state of Prussia was separated from Germany. Danzig—a Prussian port city where many German-speaking people lived—was made a free city (a self-governing unit under no nation's control). Much of Posen province was given to Poland, along with a strip of West Prussia. That strip of land came to be known as the Polish Corridor. It gave Poland access to the Baltic Sea and also separated East Prussia from Germany.

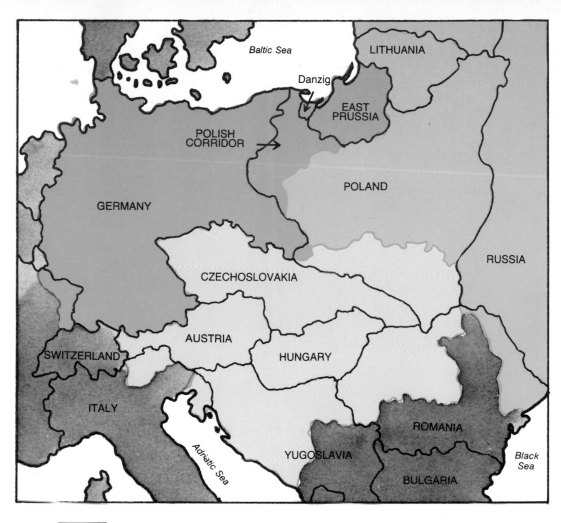

THE GERMAN EMPIRE BEFORE WORLD WAR I
THE RUSSIAN EMPIRE BEFORE WORLD WAR I
AUSTRIA-HUNGARY BEFORE WORLD WAR I
BOUNDARIES SET BY THE VERSAILLES TREATY

The Versailles Treaty also banned Germany from building any submarines or military aircraft. It limited her army to only 100,000 soldiers. And it ordered Germany to pay for all civilian damages caused by the war.

All of these terms placed a terrible financial strain on Germany. Conditions became even worse when the world plunged into an economic depression ten years after the treaty went into effect. Moreover, the treaty humiliated the proud German people. They felt its conditions were unjust and too harsh.

Already suffering from the great hardships that resulted from their defeat in World War I, Germans rioted in the streets when the worldwide depression of the 1930s caused widespread unemployment. The crowd below was demonstrating in Berlin.

In the presidential campaign of 1932, posters urging the election of
Adolf Hitler carried the Nazi slogans "Work and Bread!" and "Freedom!"
Though he lost the election to Field Marshal Paul von Hindenburg, Hitler
was able to force Hindenburg to name him chancellor on January 30, 1933.

It was during this atmosphere of defeat and
protest that Adolf Hitler came to power. Named
chancellor of Germany in 1933, Hitler very soon
afterward became an absolute dictator. He made
passionate speeches appealing to the wounded
pride of the German people. He declared that
Germany needed *Lebensraum* ("living space") to
improve her standard of living.

Almost as soon as the Versailles Treaty was signed, recruiting posters like these urged German men to join the "Free Corps" and other illegal armies that were to become the foundation of the Nazi party.

In eastern Europe and Russia lay stretches of land that would give Germany room to expand. Hitler emphasized that he was interested only in eastern Europe. All the while, despite the terms of the Versailles Treaty, he was secretly building up a huge, modern military force.

Very gradually, under Hitler's fanatical Nazi party, Germany began to stretch her muscles. In 1936, German troops reoccupied the Rhineland. In 1938, in what was called the *Anschluss* ("union"), Germany annexed Austria. And in March of 1939, Germany seized Czechoslovakia.

Left: Smiling German troops entered the Sudetenland area of Czechoslovakia after seizing the country in March, 1939.
Below: A few months after gaining control of Czechoslovakia, a triumphant Adolf Hitler waved to the crowds during a tour of the Sudetenland.

Great Britain had been somewhat sympathetic to Hitler's complaints about the harsh terms of the Versailles Treaty and his claims that Germany needed more living space. However, when Nazi Germany forced Czechoslovakia to her knees, Great Britain and her ally France were alarmed. Should Hitler turn toward the west, they would be his prime targets.

As Hitler moved east toward Russia, the Soviets became concerned. They had already suggested an alliance with Great Britain as insurance against a Nazi attack. Great Britain, despising Soviet communism, snubbed Russia.

It was logical, at least to Hitler, that the republic of Poland was next in line for a takeover. This would return Danzig (now Gdańsk, Poland) to Germany and give back Germany's freedom to move across the Polish Corridor to East Prussia.

A lone Polish soldier stands guard at the frontier during the time when Hitler was threatening to attack.

The Allied nations of Great Britain and France felt strongly that Hitler had already overstepped his power in Czechoslovakia. They warned him that they would use military force, if necessary, to protect Poland. Hitler thought the Allies were bluffing. He didn't believe they would go to war over Poland or Danzig.

The Allies' guarantee of protection, however, did encourage Poland to resist Hitler. When Hitler demanded the return of Danzig and the Polish Corridor, Poland refused.

In anticipation of an attack by Germany, Polish troops march to the front.

Hitler was outraged, but he wasn't quite ready to attack Poland. While stalling for time, he began negotiating with Russia. He didn't want Russia to join Great Britain and France in any move against his planned invasion.

While these negotiations were going on, the Polish government steadfastly refused Hitler's increased demands. Poland was banking strongly on the protection of France and Great Britain to prevent a German invasion.

"I will pounce on the Poles like lightning with mechanized forces that they don't even dream of!" shouted Hitler to a member of his high command. He had already set his own deadline for attack: September 1, 1939.

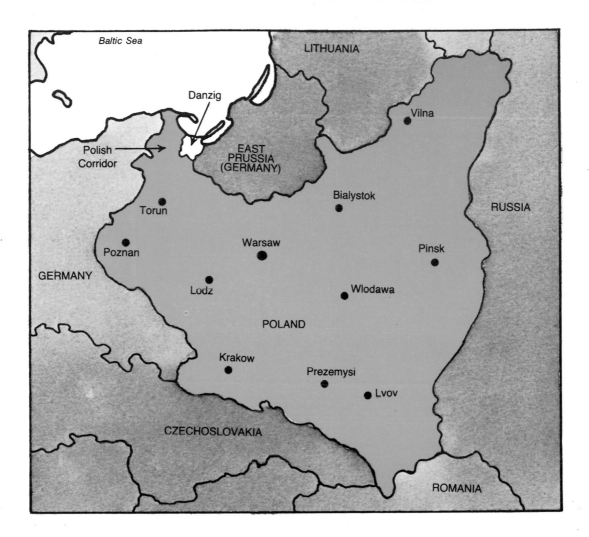

Although not fully prepared for war, Hitler looked at the situation carefully. Poland's border was very long—3,500 miles. She could be attacked from many points. To the north, south, and west of Poland lay Nazi-dominated territory. To the east lay Russia. All Hitler needed now was assurance that Russia would not interfere.

Joseph Stalin (right), dictator of Soviet Russia, stands with German Foreign Minister Joachim von Ribbentrop as Russian Foreign Minister V.M. Molotov signs the German-Russian nonaggression pact on August 23, 1939.

Finally, on August 23, Germany and Russia signed a nonaggression pact. It provided that neither country would attack the other; neither would help a third country to attack the other; and after the takeover in Poland, Germany and Russia would divide that country between them. This was all the assurance Hitler needed. He was ready to invade Poland.

On September 1, 1939, Hitler announced to the Reichstag (parliament) that he was sending German divisions into Poland. The Reichstag (above) is shown saluting the announcement.

Above: Members of the German High Command watch German soldiers cross into Poland on September 1, 1939. Also on that day, General Walther von Brauchitsch, commander of the German army, returns the salute of a subordinate officer (below) as he arrives on the Polish frontier.

This German tank regiment took part in the *Blitzkrieg* invasion of Poland.

Hitler unleashed his Nazi war machine at five o'clock on the morning of September 1, 1939. The world was about to learn a new word: *Blitzkrieg,* or "lightning war."

The invasion began with heavy air and artillery attacks. Within an hour, German troops were swarming across the Polish border. The German army was the most efficient and terrifying force the world had ever seen. On the ground were armored tanks, a variety of other vehicles, and 1.5 million soldiers. In the air were 800 high-altitude bombers, 350 dive bombers, 250 troop transports, and 250 fighter planes.

On the first day of the invasion, Polish prisoners (above) raise
their hands over their heads after being captured. A unit of German
grenade throwers (below) continues the advance into Polish territory.

A German tank regiment (above) advances into Poland and a German antiaircraft gun (below) points to the sky in case of possible Polish retaliation from the air.

This horse-drawn Polish army supply cart was typical of the out-of-date equipment in use by Poland at the time of Germany's invasion.

Poland's army and obsolete weapons were no match for this modern military machine. On the ground she had only a few light tanks and fewer than 1 million troops, many of whom had not yet been called to duty. In the air she had about 900 airplanes, most of them slow, World War I-type biplanes. The main strength of the Polish army was the cavalry—the best fighting horsemen in the world. These troops wore beautiful plumed helmets and carried sabers and lances. As splendid as they looked astride their horses, they were out-of-date and helpless against the German army of steel.

These tanks, among the few at Poland's disposal, clanked toward the front to try to stop Germany's relentless advance into the country.

There were few good roads in Poland in 1939, but its flat plains offered little resistance to the German tanks and other vehicles that streamed across the border. Two rivers in central Poland—the Vistula and the San—did provide a natural barrier. Polish troops could have stayed behind them to meet and delay the Germans. But that would have left unprotected land west of the rivers—Poland's rich farming areas, the main industrial area, and the Silesian coalfields.

Poland decided to meet Germany head-on at the border. She slammed her troops against the Nazi invaders there, hoping to delay them until help came from Great Britain and France.

The Germans had mapped out the attack well. Into the north of Poland swarmed General Fedor von Bock's Army Group—the Third Army under General Georg von Küchler and the Fourth Army under General Guenther von Kluge. Kluge rammed his troops east across the Polish Corridor, while Küchler stabbed south toward the Vistula River and Warsaw.

Meanwhile, in southern Poland, General Gerd von Rundstedt's Army Group crashed ahead in three separate flanks. The Eighth Army under General Johannes Blaskowitz was on the left; the Tenth Army under General Walter von Reichenau was in the center; and the Fourteenth Army, commanded by General Sigmund List, was on the right.

German *Stuka* dive bombers like these rained destruction on Poland during the invasion.

The German *Luftwaffe* ("air force") continued to create confusion and destruction. Their *Stuka* dive bombers ruled the air. They blew up Poland's sitting planes and airfields, destroyed railroad stations and tracks, and bombed radio stations, military headquarters, and factories. Worse, their bombs fell on open cities and killed many civilians. This destroyed Polish morale and paralyzed both the government and the military.

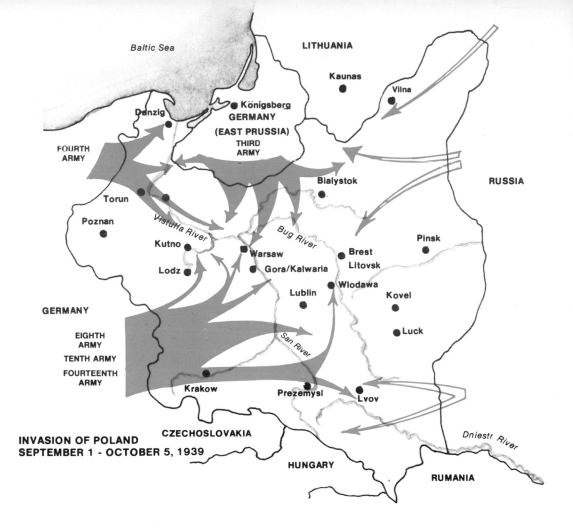

Baltic Sea

LITHUANIA

Kaunas

Vilna

Königsberg
Danzig
GERMANY
(EAST PRUSSIA)
THIRD
ARMY

FOURTH
ARMY

Bialystok

RUSSIA

Torun

Poznan

Vistula River

Kutno

Lodz

Warsaw

Bug River

Gora/Kalwaria

Brest
Litovsk

Pinsk

Wlodawa

Kovel

GERMANY

Lublin

Luck

EIGHTH
ARMY

TENTH ARMY

FOURTEENTH
ARMY

San River

Krakow

Prezemysl

Lvov

CZECHOSLOVAKIA

Dniestr River

INVASION OF POLAND
SEPTEMBER 1 - OCTOBER 5, 1939

HUNGARY

RUMANIA

The main thrust of the German attack on the south came from Reichenau's Tenth Army. He sliced across the middle of Poland with his armored divisions. To his right and left, the Eighth and Fourteenth armies were to cut off Polish forces from the north and the south. This would prevent the Poles from forming a belated defense east of their river barriers in central Poland.

Immediately, Great Britain and France demanded that Germany halt her invasion of Poland. They began to mobilize their armies. When Germany ignored their demands, the Allies declared war against her. Meanwhile, Russia sat back, watching and waiting.

World War II had begun. The German armies stormed across Poland. Within three days of the attack—as Great Britain and France were entering the war—Kluge's forces had already crossed the Polish Corridor and reached the Lower Vistula River. Küchler continued his furious pressure, bolting out of East Prussia, moving quickly and steadily toward the city of Narcy. Reichenau roared right up the center of Poland. He reached the Warta River and fought his way across. Overwhelmed, the Polish armies fell back. List hit Kracow from two sides. The Polish fighting men had no choice but to retreat from the city.

All able-bodied Poles were mobilized to help repel the German invasion. These women were full-fledged members of the Polish army.

Adolf Hitler was greeted by his victorious troops as he entered the conquered Polish city of Lodz.

Cities fell one after another. Reichenau overran and captured Tomaszow, Lodz, and Kielce. By September 8, Reichenau had reached the very outskirts of Warsaw, Poland's capital. In a single week, his army had covered 140 miles.

Battles erupted all over Poland. From every direction, German soldiers and tanks streamed forward. In the Carpathian Mountains, List overran all the troops the Poles threw at him. He crossed the area and reached the San River.

Küchler's army swept down past Narcy and fought with vicious determination against the Polish line at the Bug River north of Warsaw. Suddenly, the Polish forces found themselves trapped in a pocket west of Warsaw in the bend of the Vistula River.

As the heavy fighting rocked the country, pilots of German observation planes tried to get a true picture of the ground battles. Other aircraft continued their precision bombing and strafing of the Polish forces.

German General
Gerd von Rundstedt,
commander of
Army Group South.

The German High Command, studying the progress of the invasion, became convinced that most remaining Polish forces had scrambled across the Vistula and were now east of the river. They ordered Reichenau to cross the river and attack the Poles as they retreated.

But on the actual field of battle, things looked much different. Especially to Rundstedt. He was convinced that the majority of the Polish army was still west of the river.

He reported his convictions to the German High Command. They disagreed and an argument broke out. Finally, the High Command yielded to Rundstedt.

In those areas of Poland that were German before the end of World War I,
Hitler's invasion was welcome. Crowds of Nazi supporters in the city
of Danzig (above) salute Hitler's victorious procession through the streets.
Germans in another area of Poland (below) offer their "liberators" a cool drink.

Rundstedt was right. Because of new orders issued to Reichenau, the German invaders killed or captured most of the trapped Polish troops. Now Reichenau only had to hold his ground and wait for Blaskowitz and Kluge to join him.

By this time the Polish army had almost fallen apart. Some Polish soldiers retreated. Others attacked the Germans who happened to be nearest them. Everything was in confusion.

And still there was no help from Great Britain or France. Even though both countries were now at war with Germany, they did almost nothing to stop the Nazi advance. France could have attacked western Germany, but did not. Great Britain could have sent bombers and warships, but did not. Instead, France sent a few troops into areas already evacuated by the Germans; Britain dropped antiwar leaflets on Germany.

The reasons for this lack of support are debated yet today. France's army was trained for defensive, not offensive, fighting. It was very slow in getting organized. Britain had a strong navy, but a less-powerful air force and army. Also, because the British had many colonies, their troops were scattered all over the world. The leaders and military commanders of both countries seemed unable to agree on what to do. Their indecision would cost Poland dearly.

On September 10, a general retreat was ordered by commanders of the Polish army. They scrambled into southeast Poland, where they hoped to set up another line of defense. They had forgotten one thing, however. Russia sat waiting patiently only a few miles to the east.

On September 17, Russian troops poured across the Polish border. A knife had been stabbed in the back of struggling Poland. Now the scattered Polish forces were fighting both Germans and Russians. Enemy forces came at

These Polish prisoners of war probably were being marched off to death or interment in one of Hitler's concentration camps.

them from all sides. Although the strain of fighting was telling on the Germans, the Poles could not take advantage of this. Artillery shells continued to scream. Bombs continued to devastate the land and the people.

The prisoners taken by the Germans were shot or hanged or, sometimes worse, sent to Nazi concentration camps, where death could be—and usually was—slow and agonizing.

German troops had to fight on foot through the streets
of Warsaw, which had been blockaded with streetcars.

Despite overwhelming odds, gallant Polish
soldiers and civilians in Warsaw continued to
resist. They blockaded the city streets with
streetcars to prevent German tanks from
entering. The German soldiers were forced to
fight on foot. They had to take Warsaw block by
block and street by street. Everywhere Polish
snipers fired on the invaders. The Poles knew
that help could not arrive in time to save their
country. Still they strained to hold back the
German invaders.

Above: German troops advance through Warsaw behind the protection of a tank.
Below left: Polish troops head for the trenches outside Warsaw.
Below right: Polish troops in armored cars rumble through a village on the outskirts of Warsaw as they advance to meet the enemy in the capital city.

Dejected Polish soldiers congregated on a Warsaw street after the city surrendered.

The fight was hopeless. On September 28, 1939, the garrison at Warsaw collapsed. Although small pockets of resistance remained, Poland as a nation had been crushed.

The victorious Germans met the advancing Russians on Polish soil and divided the spoils of war. Each took over that part of Poland nearest its own border.

Adolf Hitler had talked often and convincingly of "living space." But now the space he had taken by force was filled with death, not life. No one knows exactly how many Poles died in the invasion, but the Germans captured 450,000 and the Russians 200,000. Later, 10,000 Polish officers were found buried in a mass grave, victims of the Katyn massacre. Only 14,000 Germans had been killed and 30,000 wounded.

It had taken Germany less than one month to conquer Poland. Adolf Hitler was elated and jubilant. And the world was horrified. The Nazi war machine seemed too powerful to stop. *Blitzkrieg* had led to Poland's total and rapid defeat. The German mobile armor units provided for swift, deadly troop movements. Their tactical modern air power created shock in the rear troops and disrupted both communications and the evacuation of civilians.

WALKA TRWA

IAA-1

zwyciężymy!

WYDAWNICTWO „WIADOMOSCI POLSKICH"

Opposite: German officers take a sightseeing tour of Warsaw in a bicycle-taxi propelled by a Polish man.

Polish patriots in Nazi-occupied Poland, at the risk of death or a concentration camp, found many ways to fight for their country. Some published underground newspapers that carried news and encouragement to their enslaved countrymen. An issue of the *Walka Trwa* (the Fight Goes On) carried a picture captioned "We Will Win" (left). Other Poles joined the guerrillas of the Polish Home Army and fought behind German lines. The group shown below, some of whom wore captured German uniforms, were planning an expedition with their commanding officer.

After the invasion, Hitler presented medals to the leaders of the Polish campaign. Shown here (left to right) are Generals Halder, Guderian, Hoth, Straub, Hopner, and Olbricht.

The defeat of Poland was a preview of the war to come. The *Blitzkrieg* would be used again and again. France, Belgium, and Holland were destined to fall under the might of Hitler's army. And Russia, Germany's ally during the invasion of Poland, soon would find herself fighting off a German attack.

Poland, for whose sake World War II was begun, was its hardest-hit victim. One of every 19 Poles was killed during the war and 90 percent of the 3.3 million Polish Jews were murdered.

The horrors generated by Adolf Hitler's Nazi war machine were just beginning.

Adolf Hitler, in the passenger seat, departs Warsaw after a victory parade.

Warsaw was a ruined city by the end of the war. A cross made
from charred beams is about the only evidence that this rubble
was once a church—the oldest in the city.

Index

Page numbers in boldface type indicate illustrations.

About the Author

A native of Alabama, G.C. Skipper has traveled throughout the world, including Jamaica, Haiti, India, Argentina, the Bahamas, and Mexico. He has written several other children's books as well as an adult novel. Mr. Skipper has also published numerous articles in national magazines. He is now working on his second adult novel. Mr. Skipper and his family live in Glenside, Pennsylvania, a suburb of Philadelphia.